YOU MIGHT BE FROM NEWFOUNDLAND AND LABRADOR IF...

Michael de Adder

Foreword by Mark Critch

MacIntyre Purcell Publishing Inc.
194 Hospital Rd.
Lunenburg, Nova Scotia
B0J 2C0
(902) 640-3350

www.macintyrepurcell.com
info@macintyrepurcell.com

Printed and bound in Canada by Marquis.

Design and layout: Joseph Muise
Cover design: Channel Communications
Cover Photo: Canadian Press: Andrew Vaughn

De Adder, Michael, 1967-, author You might be from Newfoundland and Labrador if... / Michael de Adder.

ISBN 978-1-927097-89-2 (pbk.)

1. Newfoundland and Labrador--Social life and customs--Caricatures and cartoons. 2. Canadian wit and humor, Pictorial. 3. Comic books, strips, etc. I. Title.

FC2161.3.D4 2015   971.8   C2015-903117-6

MacIntyre Purcell Publishing Inc. would like to acknowledge the financial support of the Government of Canada through Department of Canadian Heritage (Canada Book Fund). We are pleased to work in partnership with the Province of Nova Scotia to develop and promote our creative industries for the benefit of all Nova Scotians.

FOREWORD

Newfoundlanders love to talk. It's what we do best. The average person will speak 860,541,500 words in their lifetime. The average Newfoundlander, however, will speak 987,852,789 words before they die. I don't know if that's true. I made it up because Newfoundlanders also love to lie.

People always ask me, "Why are Newfoundlanders so funny?" I always say that as an island, and as the last to join Canada, we are like an outsider looking in. The outsider can see things that the insider has grown blind to.

Michael de Adder isn't from Newfoundland. He's what we would call a 'Come From Away.' But he is more than that. His cartoons in this book reveal more about our island in a few nuanced pen strokes than a Newfoundlander could say in a billion words. You'll laugh, you'll nod and smile, and you may even cry. Michael de Adder is not from here, but he should be. He's that good.

Newfoundland has been the butt of jokes before. Mr. de Adder never stoops to caricature or low blows. A bad cartoon is instantly forgettable and obvious. Michael's work stays with you and gets even better with multiple viewings. There are no 'Newfie jokes' here. Instead, he captures much of the magic that has made us cling to a rock in the Atlantic Ocean.

Newfoundland has terrible weather. Our soil is as deep and fertile as a tray of kitty litter. We have seen sealing and wartime disasters and economic ruin; we've lost our nationhood and have seen our young people leave the rural communities that are the cultural lifeblood of our province; but we've also become a 'have' province.

We have the top-rated restaurant in the country. We have platinum selling musicians and award-winning comedians. Hollywood films are set in the tiniest of bays. And the world's elite pay top dollar to spend the night in Fogo.

We are a bi-polar province. People ask me to explain Newfoundland to them. They ask, "What's so special about the place?" From now on, I'll just give them a copy of this book. A wise man once said "a picture is worth a thousand words." I bet buddy was a Newfoundlander.

God guard thee, Newfoundland.

— *Mark Critch*

INTRODUCTION

This book is the hardest thing I have ever done in my life. This was my Mount Everest. Or, should I say, this was my Mount Caubvick, the highest point in Newfoundland and Labrador.

You Might Be From Newfoundland and Labrador If… is the fifth book of my career and the third book in my Atlantic Canada series.

The first book was *You Might Be From Nova Scotia If…*, and it was very successful. I'm not from Nova Scotia, so I'm technically a come-from-away in that province. But my parents were both born in Nova Scotia and growing up I spent a lot of time there. I've also called it home now for more than twenty years, so I was quite at ease writing about Nova Scotia.

With my second book, *You Might Be From New Brunswick If…*, I was even more at home. I'm from Riverview, New Brunswick, so I know what it's like to be from that province.

I can tell a New Brunswicker what it's like to grow up in New Brunswick without reserve. I can even tell a Nova Scotian what it's like to grow up in Nova Scotia, as I grew up there part of the time.

What I can't do is tell a Newfoundlander what it's like to grow up in Newfoundland and Labrador.

So I didn't.

I let the people of Newfoundland and Labrador tell me what it was like to grow up in the most distinct province in Canada. I was simply just along for the ride.

I couldn't have done this book without Bill and Sharon Graham. They took time of out their lives to show me as much of Newfoundland and Labrador as we could fit in. It wasn't merely a sightseeing adventure; it was a cultural immersion. Bill and Sharon not only showed me Newfoundland, they showed me its soul.

Bill and Sharon were kind enough to introduce me to two other generous people, Gary and Ruth Green. We covered everything from mummers and music to geology and bakeapple jam. They could have written this book. In fact they could have written this book, illustrat-ed it, then written the musical version and performed it live. They are two of the most talented and interesting people I've ever met.

I'd like to thank the people at the Crow's Nest for letting me listen to its stories. I fell in love with that place as much as I fell in love with Newfoundland and Labrador, so much so that I'm now a member. One of these days I'm going to show up for a mess dinner.

I'd like to thank Marlene Leyte and Shelly Furlong for a con-versation about growing up in Newfoundland that was as funny as any conversation I've ever had. It was a time. Thanks also for letting me run ideas by you.

I'd like to thank the two guys I talked to on George St. who were smoking cigarettes. I never knew there was so much I didn't know about Vienna Sausages. I lost their names, but good luck in California.

I'd like to thank Trena Slaunwhite and Jilian Hand for the chance meeting in Petty Harbour and the screeching in. Long may your big jib draw.

I'd like to also thank Greg Little for being an excellent brainstorm-er and for offering up ideas whenever he thought of something. And for asking his parents, Anne and Gray Little, for their recollections.

I'd like to thank Meredith MacKinlay for checking me gram-mar, ,, punctuation: . annd speling. And for being a friend.

I'd like to thank Dawn Chafe for making this a better book. And Lori Summers Ford, Jerry West, Diane Paquette, Chris Smith, Wanda Baxter, Jenny Gray, Dan Frid and Geoff Brown for playing small roles that were in fact big contributions.

And I'd like to thank Mark Critch for his kind words in the Foreword. I read his quote "Michael de Adder is not from here but he should be" at the end of a long, sometimes emotional jour-ney. I was in the final days of the book and it came at the perfect time. It may be the greatest compliment I have ever received.

And a special thanks goes to Gail, Meaghan and Bridget for letting me take time out of our lives to finish yet another book. It's done.

— *Michael de Adder*

FOR DAVID

YOU MIGHT BE FROM NEWFOUNDLAND AND LABRADOR IF...

YOU KNOW IT AIN'T CALLED "THE ROCK" FOR NO REASON.

THIS WAS THE SMARTEST THING NEWFOUNDLAND EVER DID
OR THE BIGGEST MISTAKE IT EVER MADE.

YOU'RE ALWAYS A HALF-HOUR AHEAD, BUT YOUR SHOWS
ALWAYS START A HALF-HOUR BEHIND.

THE BEST PART OF A COD
IS THE TONGUE.

YOU THINK JIGG'S DINNER
TASTES BETTER ON SUNDAY.

YOU KNOW THERE'S NOTHING LIKE NEWFOUNDLAND AND LABRADOR
IN THE SUMMER.

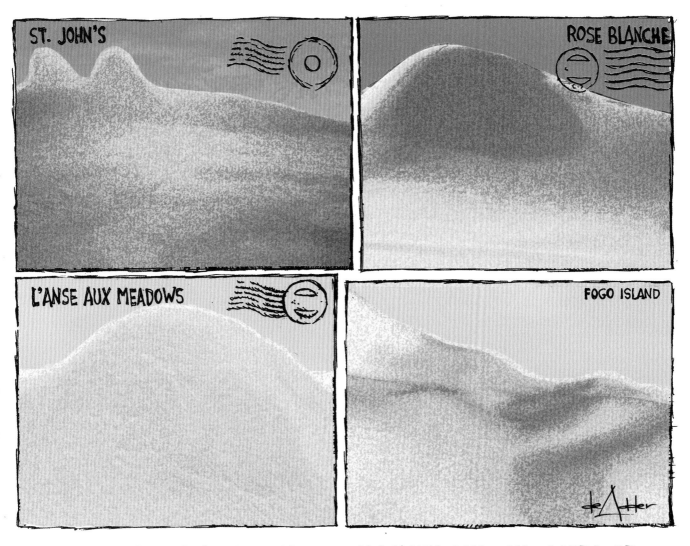

YOU KNOW THERE'S NOTHING LIKE NEWFOUNDLAND AND LABRADOR
IN THE WINTER.

YOU CONSIDER THIS THE END OF CANADA OR THE START OF CANADA,
DEPENDING ON WHICH WAY YOU ARE GOING.

YOU KNOW CHRISTOPHER COLUMBUS WASN'T THE
FIRST EUROPEAN TO DISCOVER NORTH AMERICA.

THESE GIVE YOU A SENSE OF PRIDE.

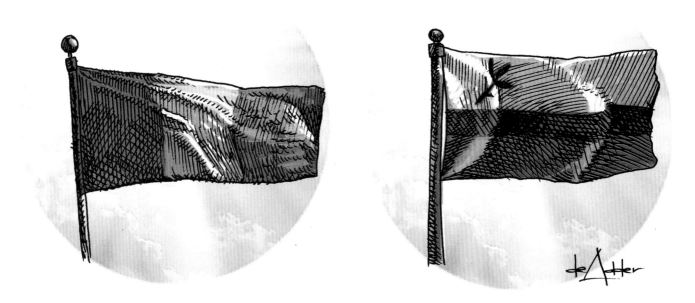

THESE ALSO GIVE YOU A SENSE OF PRIDE.

YOU'VE CAMPED IN A GRAVEL PIT.

THE HARBOUR GOT CLOGGED BY AN ICEBERG.

THE PARTY IS IN THE KITCHEN...

...UNLESS THE PARTY IS IN THE SHED.

THERE'S NOT MUCH LEFT AFTER YOU'VE GOTTEN A HOLD OF A LOBSTER.

HELPING YOUR MOTHER SORT AND CLEAN THE BAKEAPPLES
WAS A BIGGER JOB THAN PICKING THEM.

IT WAS A NICE DAY FOR CLOTHES.

YOU WALKED ON THE EARTH'S MANTLE.

YOU HAVE A WIDE RANGE OF WAYS TO ADDRESS PEOPLE.

YOU'VE GOT MANY USES FOR THE WORD "ARSE."

THESE TASTE LIKE GROWING UP.

YOU BROKE YOUR TEETH EATING BREAD.

YOU HAVE A BIG DOG.

YOU WERE THERE FOR THE FIRST MILE.

YOU DON'T NEED A STAIRCLIMBER IN ST. JOHN'S.

FRED'S RECORDS IS ON YOUR LIST OF STOPS.

FOR YOU JULY 1ST ISN'T JUST CANADA DAY,
IT'S ALSO MEMORIAL DAY.

YOU WILL NEVER FORGET THE OCEAN RANGER.

YOU DON'T KNOW WHICH ONE OF THESE YOU'RE GOING TO EAT LAST, BUT YOU KNOW WHICH ONE YOU'RE GOING TO EAT FIRST.

FISH AND BREWIS
WITH SCRUNCHIONS
HARD BREAD
SALT COD
SALT PORK

YOU HAS TO HAVE SCRUNCHIONS WITH
YOUR FISH AND BREWIS.

YOU KNOW PUFFINS REGULARLY MIGRATE
LONG DISTANCES IN LARGE PACKS.

YOU KNOW NEWFOUNDLANDERS REGULARLY MIGRATE
LONG DISTANCES IN LARGE PACKS.

YOU WERE BLOWN OFF THE HIGHWAY IN WRECKHOUSE.

YOU WELCOMED THE WORLD INTO YOUR HOME ON 9-11.

IF THERE SEEMS LIKE THERE'S NO END TO THE RAIN.

IF THERE SEEMS LIKE THERE'S NO END TO THE SNOW.

YOU PUT ALL KINDS OF CRAZY THINGS IN BOTTLES.

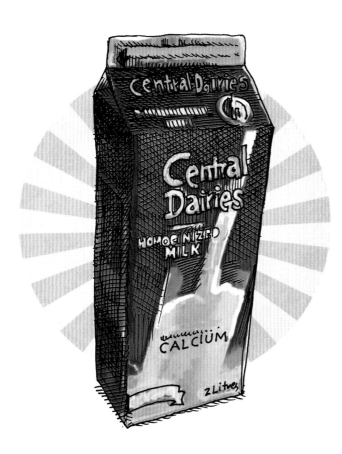

THIS IS FRESH MILK.

THIS IS TIN MILK.

YOU LIKED TO COPY PANS UNTIL THAT DAY YOUR MOTHER FOUND OUT.

YOU NOT ONLY WELCOME PEOPLE WITH MASKS INTO YOUR HOME, YOU OFFER THEM DRINKS.

THIS IS THE SHINING STAR OF THE GRANITE PLANET.

IF BUDDY TOUCHES YOUR BLUE STAR, YOU'LL KNOCK 'IM UPSIDE THE HEAD.

THIS IS THE CHAMPAGNE
OF NEWFOUNDLAND BEERS. ←

YOU CALL THIS
HORSE POWER
OR PONY PISS,
DEPENDING IF
YOU LIKE IT. →

50

YOU KNOW THIS IS FOR NEWFOUNDLANDERS ONLY.

YOU LOOK FOR THESE TO MARK TOWNIES.

PEOPLE SAY YOU TALK TOO QUICKLY, BUT
YOU THINK THEY HEAR TOO SLOWLY.

YOU CREATIVELY TAKE THE LORD'S NAME IN VAIN.

TOWN

WHEN YOU SAY YOU'RE GOING TO TOWN, YOU
REALLY MEAN YOU'RE GOING TO ST. JOHN'S.

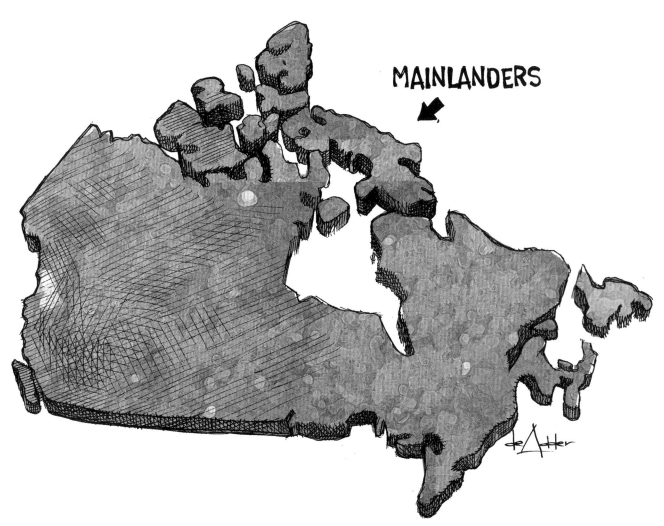

MAINLANDERS

YOU CONSIDER MAINLANDERS PEOPLE NOT FROM THE ISLAND OF NEWFOUNDLAND. (THIS CAN INCLUDE PEOPLE FROM CAPE BRETON ISLAND, PRINCE EDWARD ISLAND AND EVEN LABRADOR.)

YOUR PROVINCIAL FLOWER IS A MARSH-DWELLING CARNIVORE.

YOU MAY BE A CANADIAN, BUT
NEWFOUNDLAND IS HOME.

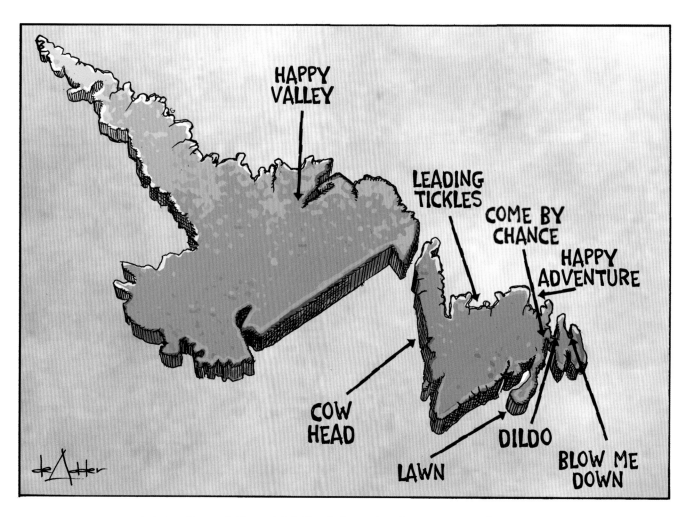

THESE ARE NORMAL PLACE NAMES.

YOU KNOW HOME IS WHERE THE HEART IS.

YOU CALL THIS AN OLD SLUT.

YOU PREFER TIN MILK IN YOUR TEA.

YOU DIDN'T HAVE A PAPER ROUTE WHEN YOU WERE YOUNG, YOU CUT OUT COD TONGUES.

YOU CONSIDER THE BEER STRIKE OF 1985 TO BE HARD TIMES.

WORLD WAR II WAS LITERALLY ON YOUR DOORSTEP.

YOU REMEMBER TAKING A TRAIN ACROSS NEWFOUNDLAND.

90% OF THE TIME YOU ANSWER "WHATTA YA AT" BY SAYING "NUTTING."

YOU GOT YOUR PICTURE TAKEN WITH A GIANT HEAD.

YOU REMEMBER WHEN NEWFOUNDLAND BECAME A HAVE PROVINCE.

YOU REMEMBER WHEN ONTARIO BECAME A HAVE-NOT PROVINCE.

YOU PUT DRESSING AND GRAVY
ON FRIES, NOT CHEESE AND GRAVY...

...AND WASH IT DOWN WITH
A TIN OF PINEAPPLE CRUSH.

YOU THINK THERE'S NO PIE LIKE SEAL FLIPPER PIE.

YOU USE "SOME" AND "RIGHT" AS MODIFYING ADJECTIVES.

THERE ARE MANY SAYINGS ONLY YOU UNDERSTAND.

YOU IDENTIFY WITH EITHER BAYMEN OR TOWNIES.

YOU CAN'T DEFINE THE WORD SKEET, BUT
YOU KNOW ONE WHEN YOU SEE ONE.

YOU'RE GOOD AT GOOD TIMES.

YOU'RE REALLY GOOD AT HARD TIMES.

YOU'RE READING THIS BOOK IN FORT MCMURRAY.

YOU GOT YOUR 15 MINUTES OF FAME
BY APPEARING ON LAND AND SEA.

YOU REMEMBER FOSTER HEWITT'S FAMOUS SIGN-ON AT THE BEGINNING OF EACH BROADCAST OF HOCKEY NIGHT IN CANADA.

OH, BABY.

BOB COLE

YOU KNOW FOR AN ENTIRE GENERATION THE VOICE OF HOCKEY WAS A NEWFOUNDLANDER.

IT'S IMPOSSIBLE TO DRESS FOR THE WEATHER.

RAIN DRIZZLE FOG

RDF IS THE WEATHER FORECAST FOR THE DAY.

YOU'RE RIGHT IN THE MIDDLE OF ICEBERG ALLEY.

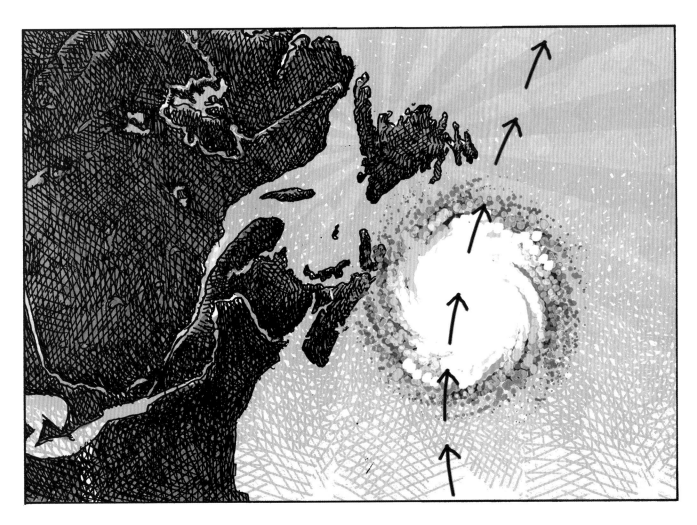

YOU'RE AT THE FAR END OF HURRICANE ALLEY.

YOU CAUGHT ENOUGH CAPELIN FOR A WEEK WITH NOTHING MORE THAN A BUCKET.

YOU PLAYED REGATTA ROULETTE AND LOST.

YOU MAKE FUN OF THE WAY PEOPLE WHO AREN'T FROM NEWFOUNDLAND AND LABRADOR PRONOUNCE NEWFOUNDLAND.

YOU TAKE GREAT PLEASURE IN WATCHING
COME-FROM-AWAYS KISS A FISH.

YOU KNOW NEWFOUNDLAND PRODUCES SOME OF THE FUNNIEST PEOPLE IN THE COUNTRY.

YOU COULD LISTEN ALL NIGHT AS GORDON PINSENT READ THE PHONE BOOK.

YOU'VE SPENT ALL DAY COOKING FOR A NEIGHBOUR IN CRISIS.

YOU GET ASKED "WHO OWNS YOU?"

YOU KNOW NEWFOUNDLAND AND LABRADOR
IS JUST AS DISTINCT AS QUEBEC.

WHEN GOING HOME YOU HAVE TO BE VERY
SPECIFIC WHEN GIVING YOUR DESTINATION.

THIS IS A NEWFOUNDLAND BAR FRIDGE.

YOU DON'T THINK THERE'S ANYTHING MISSING
FROM THESE HOMES.

YOU'RE CONSTANTLY REMINDING PEOPLE
THAT NEWFOUNDLAND AND LABRADOR IS
NOT A PART OF THE MARITIMES.

YOU LOSE YOUR MIND EVERY TIME YOU THINK OF THE RAW
DEAL NEWFOUNDLAND GOT WITH QUEBEC OVER CHURCHILL FALLS.

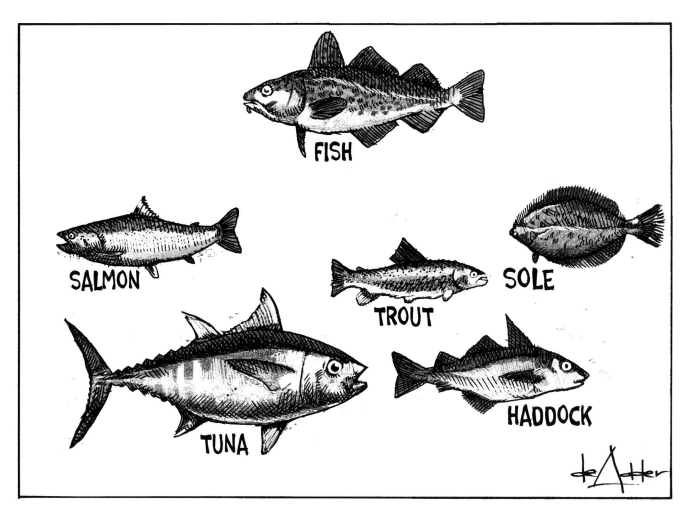

WHEN YOU SAY FISH YOU MEAN COD.

THE OLD KETTLE WAS BOILED DRY MORE THAN ONCE.

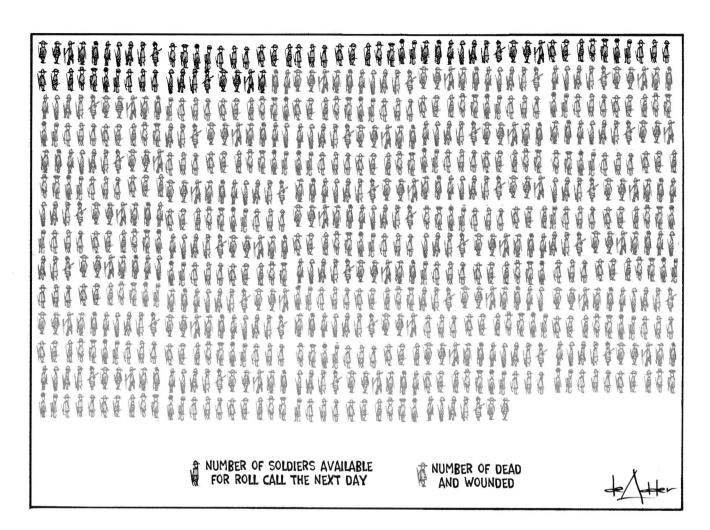

NUMBER OF SOLDIERS AVAILABLE FOR ROLL CALL THE NEXT DAY

NUMBER OF DEAD AND WOUNDED

YOU REMEMBER NEWFOUNDLAND'S LOSES AT BEAUMONT HAMEL.

YOU LOST YOUR COMMUNITY.

YOU CALL TIBB'S EVE TIPSY EVE.

YOU REMEMBER WHEN GREAT BIG SEA
WAS NOT-SO-BIG SEA.

THIS MAN'S LEGACY EVOKES STRONG EMOTIONS.

YOU'RE LESS UNCERTAIN ABOUT THIS MAN'S LEGACY.

YOU LOOKED FOR THE LETTERS S-E-X FROM ATOP SIGNAL HILL.

YOU'RE HAVING A TIME.

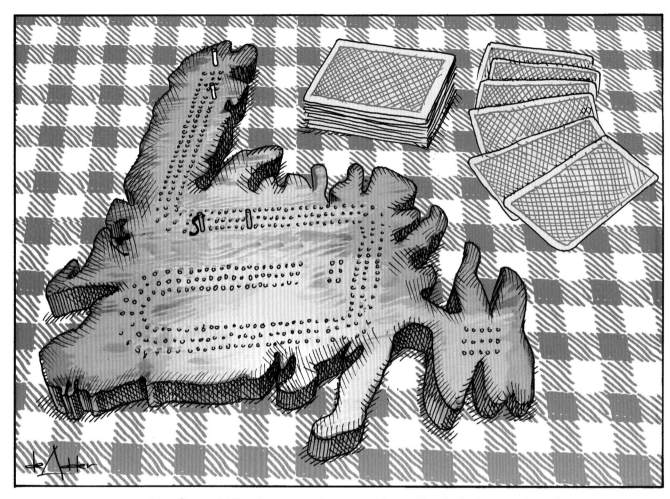

YOU'LL ONLY SEE A SKUNK IN NEWFOUNDLAND
IF YOU'RE PLAYING CRIB.

YOU GO 30 FOR 60 WITHOUT HAVING THE JACK OR THE ACE.

YOU'RE ENDLESSLY PROUD THAT NEWFOUNDLAND
HAS THE BEST RESTAURANT IN CANADA.

WHERE TO GET THE BEST FISH AND CHIPS IN NEWFOUNDLAND AND LABRADOR CAN LEAD TO A HEATED ARGUMENT.

YOU PRIDE YOURSELF ON HAVING
AN ACCURATE BULLSHIT DETECTOR.

YOU SHOVELLED OUT THE SNOWMOBILE FIRST.

YOU GOT DIRECTIONS SHOWING THE RIGHT
WAY TO GO HOME WITHOUT USING AN APP.

YOU REMEMBER THE DAY EVERYTHING CHANGED.

A PROVINCIAL TOURISM COMMERCIAL
MADE YOU TEAR UP A BIT.

YOUR EXTENDED FAMILY IS
AN ENTIRE COMMUNITY.

POLICE ISSUED A POLAR BEAR WARNING.

YOU SAID YOU SAW THE OLD MAN IN THE MOUNTAIN
EVEN THOUGH YOU DIDN'T.

THE PARTY ON GEORGE ST. ONLY GOT STARTED AT 12:00AM.

YOU VAGUELY REMEMBER HAVING FRENCH FRIES LAST NIGHT.

HISTORY REMINDS YOU HOW DANGEROUS NEWFOUNDLAND'S ICEBERG ALLEY CAN BE.

THIS SIGN REMINDS YOU HOW DANGEROUS
NEWFOUNDLAND AND LABRADOR'S HIGHWAYS CAN BE.

YOU DON'T KNOW WHY, BUT FOOD TASTES BETTER AT A BOIL UP.

ENDNOTES

Page 7. Newfoundland is the biggest island in the area so it is called "The Rock." And it's pretty much made of rock.

Page 8. Joey Smallwood signing Newfoundland into Confederation in 1949.

Page 9. Newfoundland has its own time zone.

Page 10. Technically, cod tongues are the tongue and cheeks of a cod fish dredged in flour and deep fried. Yum!

Page 11. Jiggs dinner is also called boiled dinner and is traditionally eaten on Sunday.

Pages 12 & 13. Summers are short and winters are long. Everybody would live there if this wasn't the case.

Page 14. Cape Spear, Newfoundland and Labrador, is the furthest point east in all of Canada.

Page 15. Vikings visited Newfoundland half a millennium before Columbus.

Page 16. The flag of Canada and the flag of Newfoundland and Labrador.

Page 17. The Newfoundland Tricolour and the flag of Labrador.

Page 18. Camping in old unused gravel pits was quite common.

Page 19. When it comes to viewing icebergs, Newfoundland and Labrador is one of the best places in the world. [This is Old Bonaventure]

Pages 20 & 21. Kitchen parties are famous in Newfoundland and Labrador.

Page 23. Bakeapples are wonderful if you have the patience.

Page 25. Tablelands, Gros Morne, Newfoundland and Labrador

Pages 28 & 29. I could have drawn about 10 more cartoons on Purity Products including Syrup, Lemon Creams, Ginger Cookies, Sweet Bread, Classic Milk Lunch, and various candies.

Page 34. Memorial Day is July 1 in honour of the soldiers lost at Beaumont Hamel on July 1, 1916.

Page 35. The Ocean Ranger was an offshore drilling platform which sank in the Grand Banks of Newfoundland on February 15, 1982. There were 84 crew members lost on that day.

Page 36. Vienna Sausages – it's pretty obvious which one comes out first.

Page 40. Wreckhouse, Newfoundland and Labrador, is one of the windiest places on earth, it has been said.

Page 41. Gander had 38 international flights diverted to its airport on 9–11, second only to Halifax. Gander at that time had a population of only 10,000 residents.

Page 45. Tin milk is also called canned milk.

Page 46. Pans are floating ice chunks. Copying pans is copying jumping on the same pans as the person in front of you. Clearly not something your mother would approve of.

Page 47. Mummering is a Christmas tradition where neighbours disguise themselves and house-visit people in the community. Music and noise-making is a big part of the tradition.

Page 52. Talk too quickly:
Where you 'longs to? [Where are you from?]
Give us a bit of dat luh. [Give us a bit of that love.]
'Ow she be getting on, b'y? [How is it going?]
Isn't dat foolish. [Isn't that foolish.]
I'll be over there, d'once. [I'll be over soon.]
What's after happenin' now? [What just happened?]

Page 56. Pitcher plant

Page 60. Old slut is semi-archaic now for old tea kettle.

Page 62. It was quite common for kids to cut out the tongues of the cod from fishermen returning to harbour. They'd then sell the tongues for money.

Page 63. The beer strike in Newfoundland lasted from April to November in 1985. During this period no Newfoundland beer was produced and the liquor board was forced to import American beer, which everybody hated.

Page 64. German submarine U-190 surrendered to the Royal Canadian Navy at the end of World War II and was taken to the Dominion of Newfoundland.

Page 65. Passenger service with the Newfoundland Railway started in 1898 and lasted until 1969.

Page 67. Joey's Lookout overlooking the town of Gambo. Gambo was the birthplace of Joseph R. Smallwood.

Page 68. November 2008 Newfoundland became a have province.

Page 69. In 2009–2010 Ontario became a have-not province.

Page 73. There are many saying only you understand:
Arn? [Are there any fish over there?]
Narn. [No.]
It's a mausey day. [It's a dreary wet day.]
Stay where you're to, 'til I come where you're at. [Stay there, I'm on my way.]
Long may your big jib draw. [Good fortune to you in life.]
Oh me nerves, ye got me drove! [You're driving me crazy.]

Page 74. Baymen – Newfoundlanders not from St. John's or the surrounding area. Townies – Newfoundlanders from St. John's or the surrounding area.

Page 75. Skeet – Hard to define but their natural habitat is the Avalon Mall.

Page 80. Newfoundland was an independent dominion before 1949, when Foster Hewitt said this.

Page 86. The annual capelin run which happens around June each year.

Page 87. Regatta roulette. Having drinks the night before the Royal St. John's Regatta is a gamble because the holiday can be called off on account of weather.

Page 89. Getting screeched in.

Page 90. From left to right starting at the top: Shaun Majumder, Tommy Sexton, Rick Mercer, Mark Critch, Andy Jones, Greg Malone, Mary Walsh and Cathy Jones.

Page 97. The stairs [bridge] are missing. Also know as the mother-in-law door.

Page 98. The Maritimes are New Brunswick, Nova Scotia and PEI only. When you include Newfoundland and Labrador in this group, it is collectively known as Atlantic Canada.

Page 99. 1969 Churchill Falls contract between Newfoundland and Labrador and Quebec. Quebec will get a supply of cheap power until August 31, 2041.

Page 102. The Battle of Beaumont Hamel. The next morning only 68 soldiers reported for duty. But the actual number of casualties is uncertain and changes depending on the source. The number I went with in the end was 619 casualties from the Royal Newfoundland Regiment website. So the total number of soldiers committed to battle is not represented in the illustration. That number is 721 [34 more than depicted in the illustration].

Page 103. Resettlement 1954–1975

Page 104. Tibb's Eve –The first night during Advent when alcohol was allowed to be consumed.

Page 105. Great Big Sea (Bob Hallett, Alan Doyle and Séan McCann)

Page 106. Premier Joey Smallwood – 1949–1959, 1962–1966

Page 107. Premier Danny Williams – 2003–2010

Page 108. You can see SEX several different ways by looking at the patterns streets make across St. John's.

Page 110. There are no skunks in Newfoundland. There are no porcupines, raccoons or snakes either.

Page 111. 120s, also known as Auction or Growl. There's also a version called 45s.

Page 112. Raymonds with chef Jeremy Charles is constantly winning awards as Canada's top restaurant.

Page 117. Collapse of the Atlantic northwest cod fishery.

Page 119. Francois, Newfoundland and Labrador

Page 120. Cartwright, Newfoundland and Labrador

Page 121. Man In The Mountain, Near Cornerbrook, Newfoundland and Labrador